LUKE FALLON

I0202286

FEELINGS & REASONS & HIDDEN MEANINGS

Feelings & Reasons & Hidden Meanings

Copyright © 2011 by Luke Fallon

All rights reserved. This book or any portion thereof may not be reproduced or used in any manner whatsoever without the express written permission of the publisher except for the use of brief quotations in a book review.

ISBN 978-1-4477-6222-5

FEELINGS & REASONS & HIDDEN MEANINGS

WELCOME TO MY MIND
JUST ANOTHER
NEVER AGAIN
FAVORITES
DISPLAY OF AFFECTION
SEEKING
SMILE ON MY FACE
CONFORM
LISTENING EAR
DRUNK AND DISORDERLY
FOOTPRINTS
ONLY SO LONG
QUICK
GIVE IN
PATHETIC
RUSH
MISSED CALL
REMINDER
WHATEVER
A SMALL TWIST
ENTERTAIN ME
PULL TOGETHER
TELL THE WORLD
IDIOCY
ZOMBIE SHEEP
UNBEKNOWN
LIVING DANGEROUSLY
SO SIMPLE
BAD WEATHER
TRAPPED
DEPTH
GLASS
SPECIAL MESSAGE
NEVER HIDE
BLAME
SHADOWS OF MY MIND
APPROVAL
TIME TO GROW UP
FANTASY GIRL
PART 2
PART 3
TEMPTATION

PASSIONATE EMBRACE
TIME WILL TELL
RAGE
DEFLATED
WRESTLING WITH MY MIND
SICK
DESTINED TO BE LONELY
DRUNKEN HAZE
SAME OLD ROUTINE
PUZZLE
NIGHT OUT
WALK TO UNWIND
CAR CRASH
CHANGES
SECOND GUESSING
FINAL SAY
INVISIBLE
MEANINGLESS CONVERSATION
OUTPUT
POSSIBILITY
RESOLUTION
DANCE WITH DEATH
FLOWERS
DEPTHS OF MY MIND
GOOD OLD DAYS
BRIGHT LIGHTS
TOO LATE
DAYS
DEAL WITH IT
PERFECT PLAN
SUMMER DAYS
BEST OF ME
SET UP FOR DISAPPOINTMENT
TIME IS HERE
SOMETHING ABOUT YOU
ANESTHETIC
ARGUMENTS
SHOULDER TO CRY ON
AUTHORITY
TRIBUTE
SERVANT TO MY MIND
BURNT OUT

WELCOME TO MY MIND

Welcome to my mind

There are demons you will find

So don't go deep inside

You won't like what you find

Stick to the surface

It's where you'll find purpose

And never stray too far

Because if you go in

I cannot begin, to apologize

For the sadness and hurt

JUST ANOTHER

Just another day

Quite happy today

Just another smile

First in a long while

Just another chance

To hopefully enhance

Just another way

For me to be okay

NEVER AGAIN

Deep issue

Scared tissue

Burns on my self

Worked it through

Worked it out

Never again

FAVORITES

To pick my favorites

Isn't so easy

My mind is always changing

I like so many different things

But one thing is for certain

Throughout it all

No matter what

There is one thing I can choose

The favorite part of my life

Was my time with you

DISPLAY OF AFFECTION

Not one for public displays of affection

But that doesn't mean I don't care

I just prefer to be more subtle

Keep my fondness a little concealed

Sometimes I don't much mind

On a very rare occasion

But pretty much most of my life

My tenderness stays unrevealed

SEEKING

Desperately seeking

Your attention

Want you

To notice me

Not trying too hard

That's a given

But wanting it

All the same

SMILE ON MY FACE

A cheery soul

Smile on my face

Everything is nice

Life is going great

Nothing to lose

Everything to gain

A cheery soul

Smile on my face

CONFORM

Want to be liked
Well respected
Miss popular

Want to be liked
Then conform
To the popular

Want to be liked
Then your opinion
Don't differ

Need to be accepted
Well respected
Then conform

Need to be accepted
Not dejected
Then conform

LISTENING EAR

A listening ear

Someone to talk to

Always here

Here for you

No matter the subject

Or conversation

Here to reflect

Through pain and celebration

A listening ear

Here for you

Never forget

Here for you

DRUNK AND DISORDERLY

Drunk and disorderly

Nothing out the ordinary

Just another not sober day

Doesn't matter what you do or say

Drinking until the world seems right

Drink and puke and drink and fight

Nothing but the best for me

Or anything my eye does see

Drinking until the sun comes up

Drink until I've had enough

FOOTPRINTS

Footprints in my thoughts

Remembering where I've walked

A time to look back

To reminisce

All the good times

And the worst

ONLY SO LONG

Smiling on the outside
but misery within
two sides set to collide
despite the thick skin

Only so long can you spend
Locked inside yourself
Get sick of having to pretend
Problems on the shelf

Cracks begin to appear
only so long until you break
broken sick with fear
its now time to reawake

Emotions let loose
the healing can begin
Time to call a truce
with your outside and within

QUICK

A quick hello

How are you?

How was your day?

A quick goodbye

A quick goodnight

A quick good morning after

GIVE IN

Dirty hands
you know what you did

Try to hide
but you'll never forget

Guilty mind
You know that I know

Hiding out
and I'll never forgive

Dirty hands
Guilty Mind

Try to run
Try to hide

Never forget
I'll never forgive

One day
you'll have to
Give In

PATHETIC

Call me all the names under the sun

It wouldn't be the first time I've heard them

You call me anything that you want

Because it just goes to show you are pathetic

RUSH

In a rush

Quick to judge

Hearts to crush

Hold a grudge

Never hear

What is said

Ignorance appears

Trust your head

Jump to conclusions

Don't seek answers

No need for solutions

Your mind is made up

MISSED CALL

One missed call

A dumb mistake

Forgot to charge my phone

I wish I hadn't

Knew I should of

I tried to get in touch

There was no answer

Such a shame

I hope you call me back

One missed call

Led to another

I hope it doesn't keep up

REMINDER

Cut myself shaving

This scar an engraving

To remind me

To never feel free

To give you another

Chance

WHATEVER

A list of whatever

Whatever you wanted

Whatever you needed

Whatever I could give

Whatever the reason

Whatever the meaning

Whatever you want I'll give

Whatever is wrong

Whatever is right

Whatever is on your mind

Whatever the problem

Whatever the fight

Always by your side

A SMALL TWIST

Thoughts twisted

Can't think straight

Got to clean up

It's never too late

ENTERTAIN ME

Entertain me

Make me smile

Prove it's all worthwhile

Make me laugh

And let me see

What it is you want from me

Take your time

And try to be

As happy as you make me

PULL TOGETHER

Bored alone

Feelings unknown

Regrets a few

Got to start a new

Pull myself together

A new endeavor

Put my mind at ease

Myself I have to please

To make it all fine

Another chance to shine

TELL THE WORLD

Open up

Tell the world

What is up

What is down

Tell it all

And don't be shy

Let it out

Laugh and cry

Share your problems

Share your guilt

Open up

And

Tell the world

IDIOCY

Thoughtless comments

To a friend

Should have realized

I'd need to make amends

Think more

Before I speak

Learn to reveal

To only the trustworthy

A pointless thought

Is what it should have stayed

Instead I opened up

My idiocy displayed

ZOMBIE SHEEP

Clouded opinions

No thoughts of your own

Told by the masses

That you aren't alone

Following the heard

Believing the lies

Doing as they tell you

No individual in sight

Another sheep

Another zombie drone

Brain washed

By the masses

No life of your own

UNBEKNOWN

Desperation

All alone

My misery

Unbeknown

Unhappy

All alone

Depression

Unbeknown

Nothing for me

All alone

My feelings

Unbeknown

LIVING DANGEROUSLY

Living dangerously

A life on the edge

Trying vigorously

To push yourself

Living dangerously

Taking every risk

Trying so hard

For that rush

SO SIMPLE

An onerous task

Demanding work

Just to get this right

Too much effort

To spend

On something

That should be

So simple

BAD WEATHER

Bad weather

Cloudy day

Lightning storms

A spot of rain

A metaphor

For my mind

Bad decisions

Hurts inside

TRAPPED

Trapped in my head

No room to breath

Lost in my thoughts

No time to think

Confused by my mind

No clarity

Abused by my dreams

So cannot sleep

Refused by myself

For everything

A need to confirm

I still exist

DEPTH

Sadness in your eyes

Because I realize

The depth of your lies

To try an idealize

Your miserable life

GLASS

Glass half empty

Or glass half full

An age old question

Those options aren't all

The alternative

Is quite clear

That in fact

The glass is

Just too big

SPECIAL MESSAGE

I know it can't be easy being you

I can only imagine what it is you go through

It's not right and it's not fair

And for you I send this poem this prayer

I hope it can bring a smile to your face

If only for a second in your uphill race

My thoughts are with you and your situation

I'm inspired by you and your determination

NEVER HIDE

You've got a problem

So take it out on me

Though it isn't my problem

It's a conflict with you

And you should realize

That no matter what

You can try and try

But from yourself you'll

Never hide

BLAME

Blame myself

For listening to you

Blame you

For encouraging me

Blame my parents

For my existence

Blame everyone else

For everything since

SHADOWS OF MY MIND

The shadows of my mind

It's where you will remain

Deeply tucked away

With all my other pain

In a vault with no key

Locked forever more

A faraway recollection

Which it will forever be

Constantly in the shadows

The shadows of my mind

APPROVAL

I seek your approval

I know I don't have to

But it feeds my ego

Makes me think it'll all be fine

If you like what I do

It means they weren't right

If you like what I've done

Then everything is right

TIME TO GROW UP

Keep being told about responsibility
a need to grow up and take heed
to age and behave to the best of my ability
expectations too high to exceed

Cut out the comic books
no chance of that

Drink less not optional

Drugs a definite no

Grow up
take heed
responsibility

Grow up
grow old
with dignity

FANTASY GIRL

My fantasy girl

See you about town

From time to time

You'll never know it's you

But your smile and your cheer

Brightens up my day

You'll probably

Never read this

I doubt you know

I exist

But it's fun all the same

Just thinking of you

PART 2

Unnoticed in your eyes

Just another passer by

A plan I must devise

So you stop and wonder why

You never noticed my smile

Then I'll play at this a while

Until you realize

That I might just be right

PART 3

I walked passed

I saw you glance

In my direction

A cheeky grin

A smile within

Finally attention

Soon will be

The time to act

And make it all clear

That though

You don't know who I am

You soon sure will my dear

TEMPTATION

Can't resist the temptation

After all I'm only human

Feel like I should give in

The sight of you in front of me

A mistake that I'm bound to make

You're the one that I could

Never resist

PASSIONATE EMBRACE

A passionate embrace

Is not a reason to stay

It's just a distraction

To put things off for another day

To divert your mind in a trivial way

To leave you feeling happy

Until you start thinking straight

Then comes the next distraction

Could be anything really

Round and round in circles

Until the big reveal

TIME WILL TELL

Only time will tell

What is in store for us all

Only time will tell

How well we grow

Only time will tell

How this will all go

Only time will tell

If our choices were our own

Only time will tell

When we look back on it all

RAGE

A build up of rage

Anger and hate

Got to let loose

Let it all out

Tell it how it is

Consequences

No concern

Time to release

Time to let out

The time is now

Engaging

In a fury

Embrace the rage

DEFLATED

Feeling deflated

Not the situation

I'd anticipated

A good friend

Gone but never lost

Will live on

In the memories

Of those he'd touched

WRESTLING WITH MY MIND

Wrestling with my conscience

Do I tell him what I know?

How do I crush his world?

How to let him know

We are sure to fall out

Not a true good friend

Yet still it is hard

Can I leave him oblivious?

Keeping this a secret

It all comes down to my

Conscience

Grappling with my mind

SICK

Controlled me

Abused me

Took advantage

You used me

Playing your games

Testing my faith

Sick and tired

Of your games

Confused me

You lose me

Because now

I'm no use at all

DESTINED TO BE LONELY

Destined to be lonely

A life unaccompanied

Unsocial and alone

A life so solitary

Dejected lone soul

Entirely exclusive

Years just on your own

DRUNKEN HAZE

Drunken haze
Minds a blur
Lost days
situations occur

Lost moments
can't recall
meaningless arguments
feeling two feet small

Passed out
feeling shit
No doubt
deserved it

Kept my mouth closed
is what I should of done
thoughts exposed
spoiled all the fun

SAME OLD ROUTINE

Stuck in a rut

Same old routine

Feeling in the gut

Need a change of scene

Wake up

Intake of caffeine

Try to write

Get distracted by the screen

Almost sleeping

Need for more coffee

Get distracted by the TV

Rinse repeat

The same old routine

PUZZLE

Got a puzzle and it's hard to solve

in fact quite complex

Certain parts need further resolve

Definitely made to perplex

The more I stop and think about it

I can't resist trying to figure it out

Pushing pieces where they just don't fit

Trying to recognize what it's all about

Too complicated for me to understand

Some parts are missing or not all that clear

Takes too much brain power for me to command

I think I'll get there but the solution I fear

Too difficult I'm going to give in

NIGHT OUT

Cigarette smoke

And the stench of alcohol

A Laugh and a joke

Inhibitions out of control

A good night out

With a decent conclusion

A sing and a shout

A lovely drunk confusion

WALK TO UNWIND

A brisk walk to unwind

To clear what's up what's on my mind

To come to terms with the situation

To come up with a revelation

A long walk to take it all in

To work out where to begin

It's now time for me to proceed

To forgive if I wish to succeed

CARCRASH

My life I can best describe

As a car crash one hellish ride

Twisted metal and Annihilation

A scene of ruin and decimation

In need of urgent care

Bystanders just stop and stare

Aids in sight I can just about see it

Maybe it would help if I just admit

That my life is worth saving

This pain is worth braving

To get on track and believe in my self

Nurse my ego and myself back to health

CHANGES

A fear of making changes

In short Tropophobia

From our previous exchanges

No doubt describes you

Too scared to take a gamble

And lay it on the line

Too much of a scramble

Of what you know

Fixed on the illusion

You are happy how you are

Content with seclusion

No desire to take a chance

SECOND GUESSING

The situation always does arise

You have doubts question time

Second guessing my words

Never giving the benefit of the doubt

Always testing everything I say

Not letting me have my day

Questioning me every step

Never letting up never giving in

FINAL SAY

You have to have the final word

You have to say your peace

You can never let things rest

You could never resist

So have that final say

Get it off your chest

I refuse to play along anymore

Because it just become too pathetic

INVISIBLE

Developed a superpower

Turned invisible

You can't see me now

I'm a ghost

Not in you're perception

You can't see me

I'm just an illusion

A specter

A shadow

Cleverly concealed

Disappeared

From your line of sight

Unseeable to the naked eye

Hidden in the corner of your vision

JUST A SHADY APPARITION

MEANINGLESS CONVERSATION

Meaningless conversation

Just to pass the time

Some light flirtation

Advances to decline

Just a bit of fun

To make life seem less bleak

No harm done

Now to move on with my week

Not always the best

Not always so profound

I write or type what's on my mind

Sometimes it not so grand

One minute I am depressed

The next I'm filled with joy

I write it all my minds a mess

In hope that someone enjoys

POSSIBILITY

Inspired by the thought of you

Does me good just thinking it through

A possible future still very likely

Just need you to realize entirely

Tried it once wasn't the right time

Now I think it would be prime

Going to wait it through

Till you see myself with you

A friend but we could be nearer

Just waiting for the circumstances to be clearer

RESOLUTION

Understand

Gather and translate

The sights and sounds

Realize and create

A solution

Time to comprehend

Resolution

My life on the mend

DANCE WITH DEATH

A dance with death

Life flashes before your eyes

Out of breath

Caught you by surprise

Outlook reset

Now you've come to understand

Your mind is set

Now your life is not so bland

Time to live

With reason and determination

A chance to give

That dance with death your salvation

FLOWERS

My sweet buttercup

Perfect to the eye

Wanting to be close-up

Hurts to say goodbye

My gorgeous rose

Can still surprise

And it shows

I really don't like goodbyes

DEPTHS OF MY MIND

The depths of my mind

I don't like what I find

So I try hard to hide

And not delve deep inside

The depths of my mind

GOOD OLD DAYS

Long gone are the good old days

Of feeling young no feeling afraid

A long lost nearly forgotten past

When life was fun what a blast

Recent reunions not quite the same

Lacked the passion thrill and energy

Years gone it's such a shame

Oh what I would give for the good old days

BRIGHT LIGHTS

Bright lights

Drawn towards

Shining sights

Feeling good

Brilliant design

Such a delight

Vivid shine

Justified

Radiant glow

Enticed inside

Glisten blinding

A shining guide

TOO LATE

It's too late you missed your chance

The window has passed

For once I would have forgiven you

But now that is long in the past

You missed the opportunity
to spend your life with me

You walked out you gave in

Didn't have the courage to let me in

Time has come
and long passed

There is nothing more to say

You can wish and hope
all you like

But at the end of the day

You lost me

DAYS

Today is just

Tomorrows

Yesterday

Anything done

Will soon be

Forgotten

Everything is

Soon in the past

So no regrets

No point living

In the past

DEAL WITH IT

Changes in the way you act

Desperate for attention

Never one to react

To your overblown exaggerations

You lost me

Now deal with that

Because you're the one who chose

To rid yourself of me

So please don't now

Come crawling back

Because I'm done

No chance with me

You made damn sure of that

PERFECT PLAN

I dream to be

A better man

A better friend

The perfect plan

I dream of

A better life

A better future

The perfect plan

I dream to see

A better me

A better you

The perfect plan

SUMMER DAYS

Summer days

Feeling great

Sun is out

No complaints

Shining bright

Laughter's high

Summer days

Feeling great

BEST OF ME

Can't get the best of me

See right through your deceit

Lie to you to make you think

That everything is just fine

SET UP FOR DISAPPOINTMENT

You set me up for disappointment
at every twist and turn

Why can't you just be straight with me
or leave me well alone

You say you want to be just friends
and that is fine by me

But then you start all this I miss you shit
Sending mixed messages

Don't you see
Of course I miss you

And obviously I still care

But it's never quite as simple as that

You set me up for disappointment

TIME IS HERE

Tick tock

The chime of the bell

Time is up

Time to tell

Are you here?

Or are you late?

Will you ever show?

Did you decide not to come?

To stay away forever

Did you decide this is done?

If so

Farewell

SOMETHING ABOUT YOU

Something about your eyes

That makes you seem so right

Something about that smile

That makes you seem just right

Something about you

That makes you right

ANESTHETIC

I hope I can return

To a world less absurd

A world where I can voice

My overall concerns

A world where I can sleep at night

Without fear of nasty dreams

An anesthetic needed

Just to live quite simply

ARGUMENTS

Argumentative personality

Trying to get the best of me

Fighting for the sake of it

Making me feel like shit

Rational discussion

Not an option

No conclusion in sight

Can't take it again tonight

Contention and conflict

Controversy addict

An ugly debate, engagement

Disputes bitter, disappointment

There's no longer a point

Destructive feeling of disjoint

SHOULDER TO CRY ON

I can be your shoulder to cry on

Reliable, someone to confide in

I will always be here for you

No matter what you say or do

I'm no knight in shining armor

But I can listen if that's what you desire

AUTHORITY

Challenging authority

Got a voice a desire to speak

Let it out can't keep it in

Need to stand up

Let it be heard

Conflict with the powers that be

Confidence is necessary

Empowerment of the masses

No more sitting on your asses

Got a voice

And it needs to be heard

Self assurance and certainty

Control to take back you'll see

Somebody must answer me

CONFLICT WITH AUTHORITY

TRIBUTE

Inspiring words

A man long dead

Respected, Reputable

An icon, A Legend

Is this the end?

Wishful, Sinful

A wild child of sorts

Rock royalty

A superstar

This is a tribute if you will

To the man to the message

That his words do send

SERVANT TO MY MIND

The undisputable

Irrefutable

Servant to my mind

Paranoid

Feeling devoid

Nowhere left to hide

BURNT OUT

Burnt out

Nothing to write

Spent too much time

Diving in my mind

Nothing left in there

That is easy to find

Hit a wall can't get past

Can't get the juices flowing

On the backburner

For a time

Need time to refresh

Time to recollect

And recover

The depths

Of my twisted head

www.ingramcontent.com/pod-product-compliance
Lightning Source LLC
Chambersburg PA
CBHW071833020426
42331CB00007B/1717

* 9 7 8 1 4 4 7 7 6 2 2 2 5 *